Bill Evans
Plays Standards

W9-AUX-717

CONTENTS

Cover photo: Nenette Evans, © 1998

Bill Evans Estate is Administered by:
Nenette Evans
P.O. Box 7808
Laguna Niguel, CA 92607

ISBN 0-7935-7046-8

7777 W. BLUEMOUND RD. P.O. BOX 13819 MILWAUKEE, WI 53213

Visit Hal Leonard Online at
www.halleonard.com

"I want to reach the point where we can convey emotions that are higher than just everyday feelings. That's the real purpose of the music, to reach something higher, and to bring out a feeling in the listener. Then we've created worthwhile music.

You can't get there, though, by being too subjective. Jazz is not only expressing yourself, but relating to the other players and also knowing your musical materials. In order to produce music, you must be able to take it apart and analyze it. This is the challenge that most players ignore.

After that, it takes a tremendous amount of time, effort and desire to do it. The key word is desire. I've worked hard but I've never labored. It was pure pleasure."

Bill Evans interview by Richard Hadlock, San Francisco Chronicle, 1963

DISCOGRAPHY OF TRANSCRIBED PERFORMANCES

AUTUMN LEAVES, MY FOOLISH HEART, MY ROMANCE, UP WITH THE LARK - CD - TURN OUT THE STARS - THE FINAL VILLAGE VANGUARD RECORDINGS - WARNER BROS. 45925-2

GOODBYE - EMPATHY - VERVE V6 8497; CD - 837 757 - 2

HOW DEEP IS THE OCEAN - BILL EVANS TRIO LIVE - VERVE V6 8803

IN A SENTIMENTAL MOOD - CALIFORNIA HERE I COME - VERVE VE 2 - 2545

ON A CLEAR DAY - ALONE - VERVE V6 8792; CD - 833 801 - 2

All Verve recordings are also available on the CD boxed set
THE COMPLETE BILL EVANS ON VERVE - 314 527 953 - 2

BIOGRAPHY

Miles Davis said it best: "He played the piano the way it should be played."

William John Evans was born on August 16, 1929 in Plainfield, New Jersey. It was the year of the stock market crash and the beginning of the Great Depression. Bill's mother, Mary Soroka, was of Russian heritage; his father, Harry Evans, of Welsh decent. Bill also had an older brother named Harry, Jr. whom he loved and respected. Bill began piano lessons at age six, violin at seven, and flute at thirteen. He played piano in various youth groups during his high school days at North Plainfield High School, where he graduated in 1946. He entered Southeastern Louisiana College on full scholarship at age seventeen majoring in piano and graduated, with honors, in 1950. After college, Bill played briefly with Mundell Lowe and Red Mitchell in New York, then joined the Herbie Fields band.

In 1951 he joined the 5th Army Band at Fort Sheridan, Illinois, where he remained for three years. During his Army stint he often played in Chicago and gained experience playing in big bands and various-sized combos. He also played solo piano and accompanied singers. In 1954 he returned to New York and played with the top musicians of the day. Orrin Keepnews, producer for Riverside Records, signed Bill to a contract. The Bill Evans Trio (Teddy Kotick, bass and Paul Motian, drums) made their first album entitled *New Jazz Conceptions* in 1956. Bill attended the Mannes College of Music for one semester, studying composition. He wrote "Waltz for Debbie" for his niece, which was included in his first trio album. Bill continued to play and record with such musicians as Gunther Schuller, Don Elliot, Joe Puma, Hal McKusick, Charles Mingus, Jimmy Knepper, Sahib Shihab, Cannonball Adderley, Helen Merrill, and Eddie Costa.

Bill joined the Miles Davis Sextet in 1958, replacing Red Garland. He is the pianist on the classic album *Kinda Blue*. While with Davis, Bill recorded and played with other groups led by John Coltrane, Tony Scott, George Russell, Lee Konitz, Art Farmer, Bill Potts and Chet Baker. In the summer of 1959, Bill taught at the School of Jazz in Lenox, Massachusetts. Bill's stay with Davis was short, and he eventually went back to the trio format, recording the album *Everybody Digs Bill Evans*. More important albums followed.

The trio of 1959 included Bill, bassist Scott LaFaro and drummer Paul Motian. This was Bill's dream trio and set the standard for jazz piano trios for the next twenty years. Unfortunately, LaFaro was killed in an auto accident two weeks after the trio recorded *Sunday at the Village Vanguard*. Bill became despondent. But, six months later, Bill brought in bassist Chuck Israels and the Bill Evans trio continued to record and travel.

Of particular interest to pianists, as well as all musicians, were Bill's piano voicings, influenced by his interest in Ravel, Debussy and Chopin. He continued touring and recording classic albums with a variety of artists for the Verve label. The personnel of the trio changed during the years, but the imprimatur of Bill Evans remained constant. He won the American Legion Award, the Down Beat Critic's Poll (nine times), seven Grammy Awards, Jazz Magazine's Jay Award, the NARAS Lifetime Achievement Award, and was elected into the Jazz Hall of Fame at the Institute of Jazz Studies at Rutgers University. Outside of the United States, he achieved the Critic's Top Pianist Award from the Melody Maker (UK), the Edison Award (Scandinavia), and the Swing Journal Award (Japan).

Evans died on Monday September 15, 1980 at New York's Mount Sinai Hospital.
Evans' style greatly influenced such pianists as Herbie Hancock, Keith Jarrett, Chick Corea, Marc Copland, Lyle Mays, Joey Calderazzo, Kevin Hays, Kenny Kirkland, Jim McNeely, Fred Hersch, Warren Bernhardt, Billy Childs and many other contemporaries too numerous to mention. His genius lives on today.

William F. Lee III, Ph.D, Mus.D.

ON A CLEAR DAY (You Can See Forever)

from ON A CLEAR DAY YOU CAN SEE FOREVER

Words by Alan Jay Lerner
Music by Burton Lane

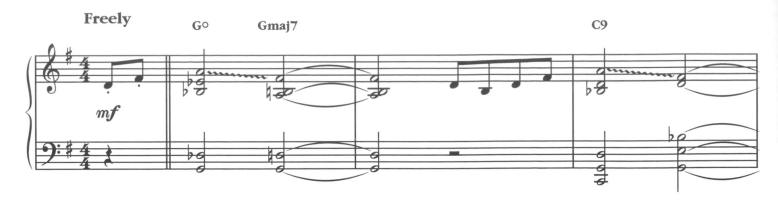

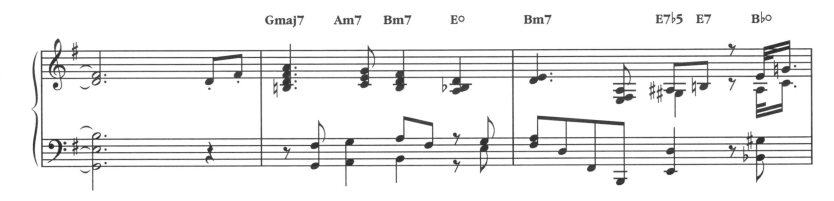

IN A SENTIMENTAL MOOD

By Duke Ellington

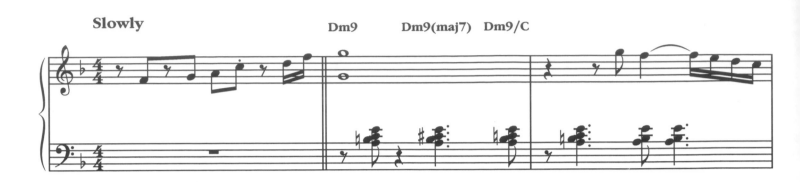

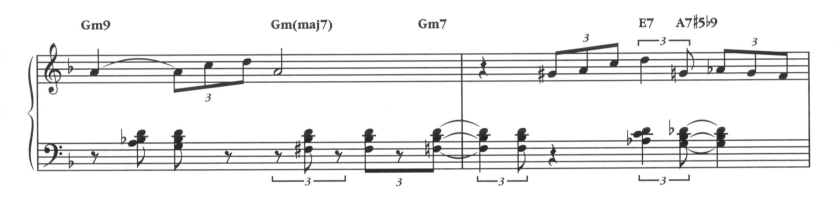

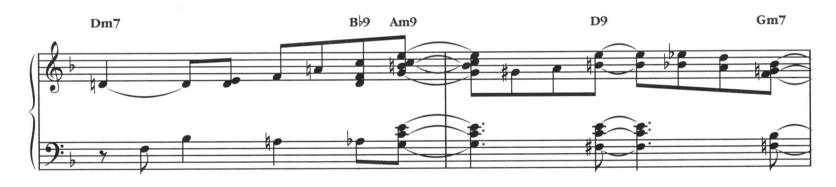

GOODBYE

Words and Music by GORDON JENKINS

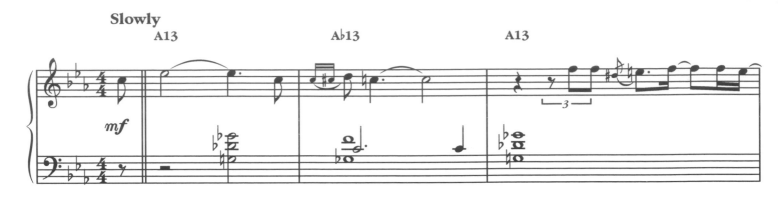

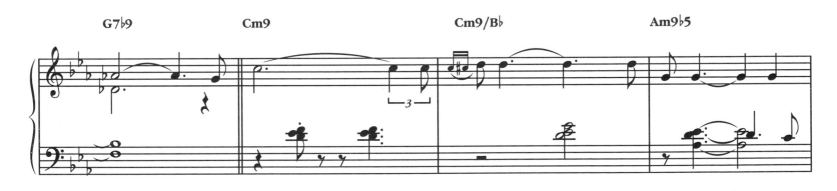

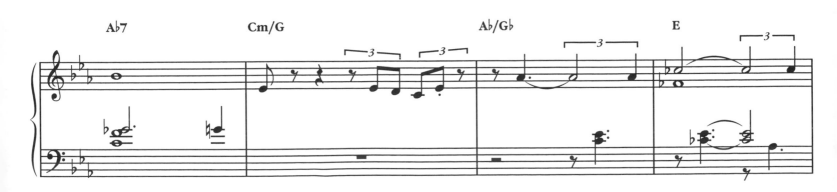

UP WITH THE LARK

Words and Music by Jerome Kern

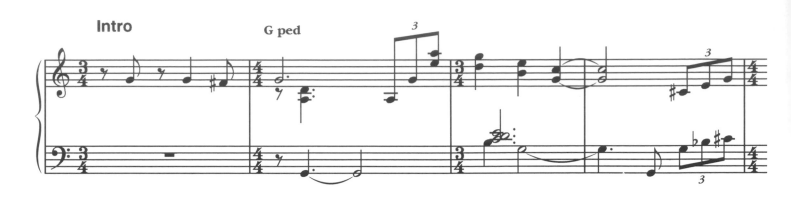

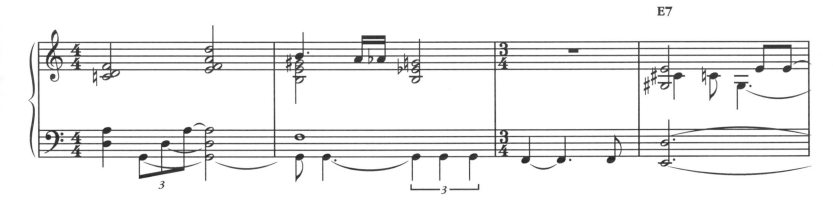

Piano Solo

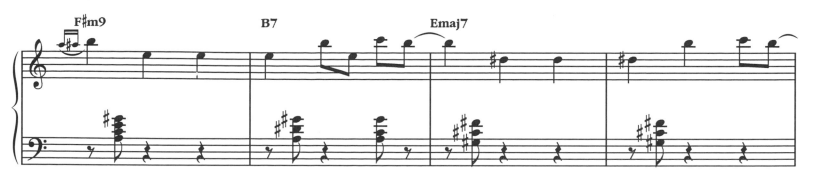

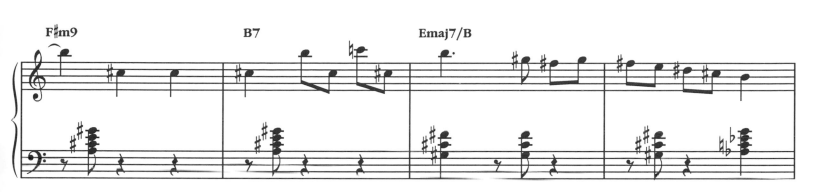

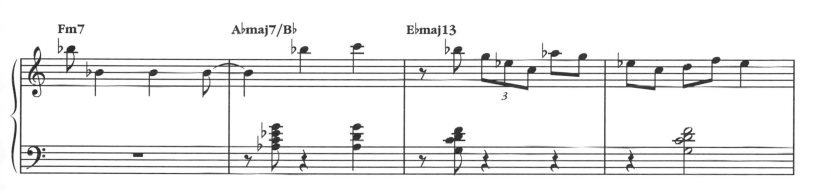

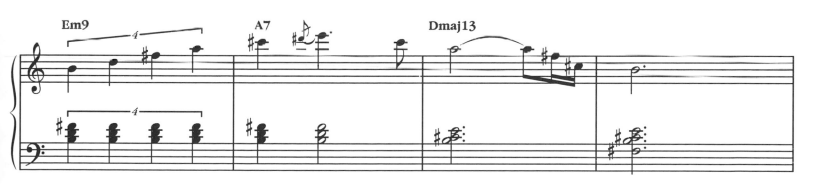

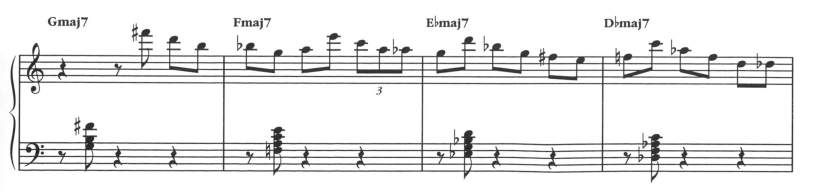

40

HOW DEEP IS THE OCEAN

(HOW HIGH IS THE SKY)

Words and Music by Irving Berlin

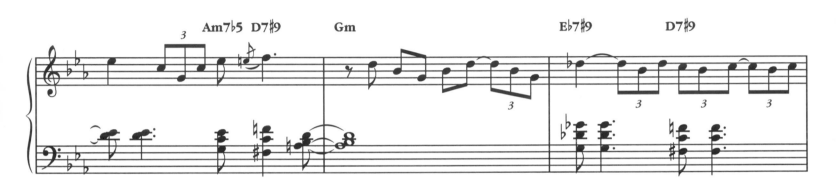

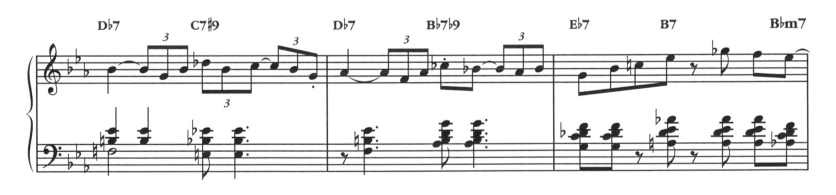

AUTUMN LEAVES

(Les Feuilles Mortes)

English lyric by Johnny Mercer
French lyric by Jacques Prevert
Music by Joseph Kosma

Piano Solo

MY FOOLISH HEART

Words by Ned Washington
Music by Victor Young

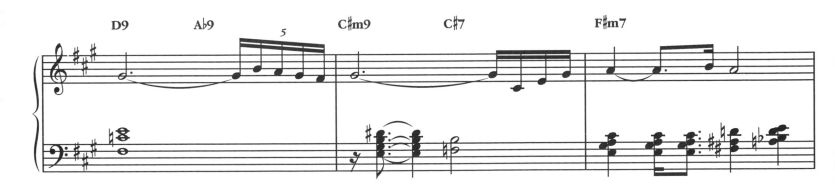

MY ROMANCE

from JUMBO

Words by Lorenz Hart
Music by Richard Rodgers

Note: 1. Before B , there are alternating drum and
bass solos - 32 bars each
2. Before C , there is a 32 bar drum solo

2nd Piano Solo